WRITE
SOURCE
My Book for Writing, Thinking, and Learning

MW00582998

WRITE SOURCE®

GREAT SOURCE EDUCATION GROUP
a division of Houghton Mifflin Company
Wilmington, Massachusetts

Written and Compiled by
Patrick Sebranek, Dave Kemper,
and **Patricia Reigel**

Illustrated by **Chris Krenzke**

Acknowledgements

We're grateful to everyone who helped develop the *Write Source* text. First, we must thank all the teachers and students from across the country who contributed ideas and writing models.

We also want to thank our Write Source/ Great Source team for all of their hard work and dedication to this project:

Steve J. Augustyn, Laura Bachman, April Barrons, Colleen Belmont, Susan E. Boehm, Evelyn Curley, Chris Erickson, Mark Fairweather, Mariellen Hanrahan, Tammy Hintz, Judy Kerkhoff, Lois Krenzke, Joyce Becker Lee, Mark Lalumondier, Michele Order Litant, Dian Lynch, Colleen McCarthy, Pat Moore, Kevin Nelson, Tracy Olson, Sue Paro, Linda Presto, Jason C. Reynolds, Susan Rogalski, Janae Sebranek, Lester Smith, Richard Spencer, Julie Spicuzza, and Jean Varley.

Photo Credits:
Page 54 Photodisc/Photodisc Blue/Getty Images

Dear Boys and Girls,

This *Write Source* book is just for you. You can write about your ideas in this book. You can also draw pictures. There is a section in the back of the book called "My Own Dictionary." That's where you can write new words you are learning.

The children inside this book will help you. You'll also meet Spot. He likes to read and write, too!

We hope you have fun writing.

Your friends at Write Source

Contents

I have a special writing spot.
It's where I **look** and **think** a lot.
It's where I **talk** and **listen**, too,
and where I **read** about what's new.

At first, my paper is plain white.
But then I start to **draw** and **write**.
I **add** some words and **check** with care.
And after that, it's fun to **share**.

My Writing Spot

Draw a picture of yourself in your writing spot.

This is my writing spot.

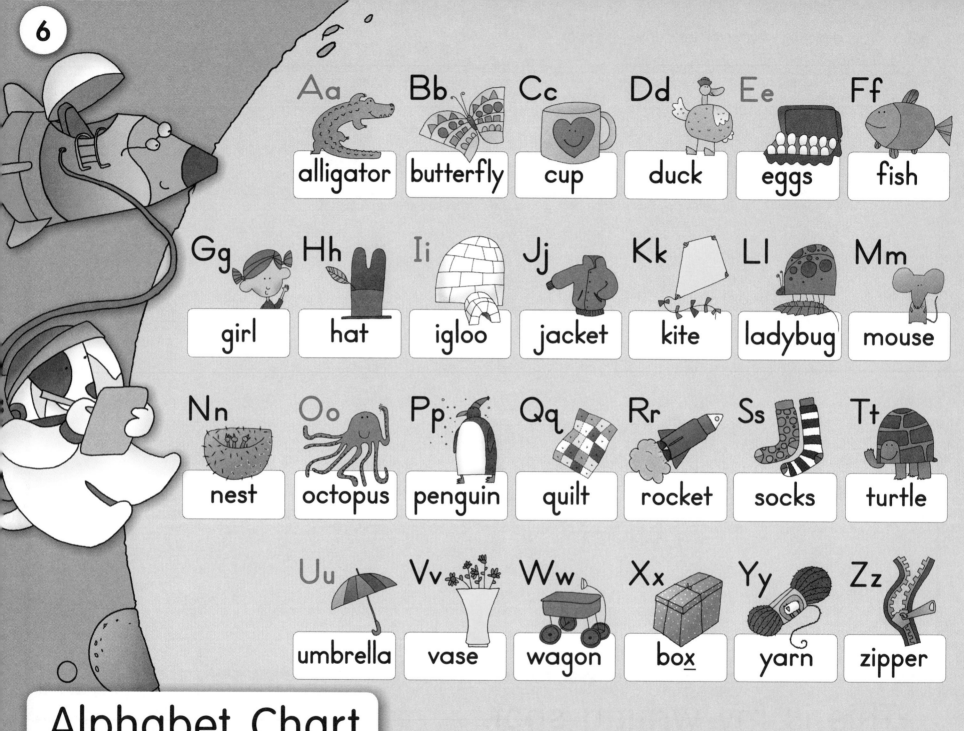

Aa alligator
Bb butterfly
Cc cup
Dd duck
Ee eggs
Ff fish

Gg girl
Hh hat
Ii igloo
Jj jacket
Kk kite
Ll ladybug
Mm mouse

Nn nest
Oo octopus
Pp penguin
Qq quilt
Rr rocket
Ss socks
Tt turtle

Uu umbrella
Vv vase
Ww wagon
Xx box
Yy yarn
Zz zipper

Alphabet Chart

I write alphabet letters.

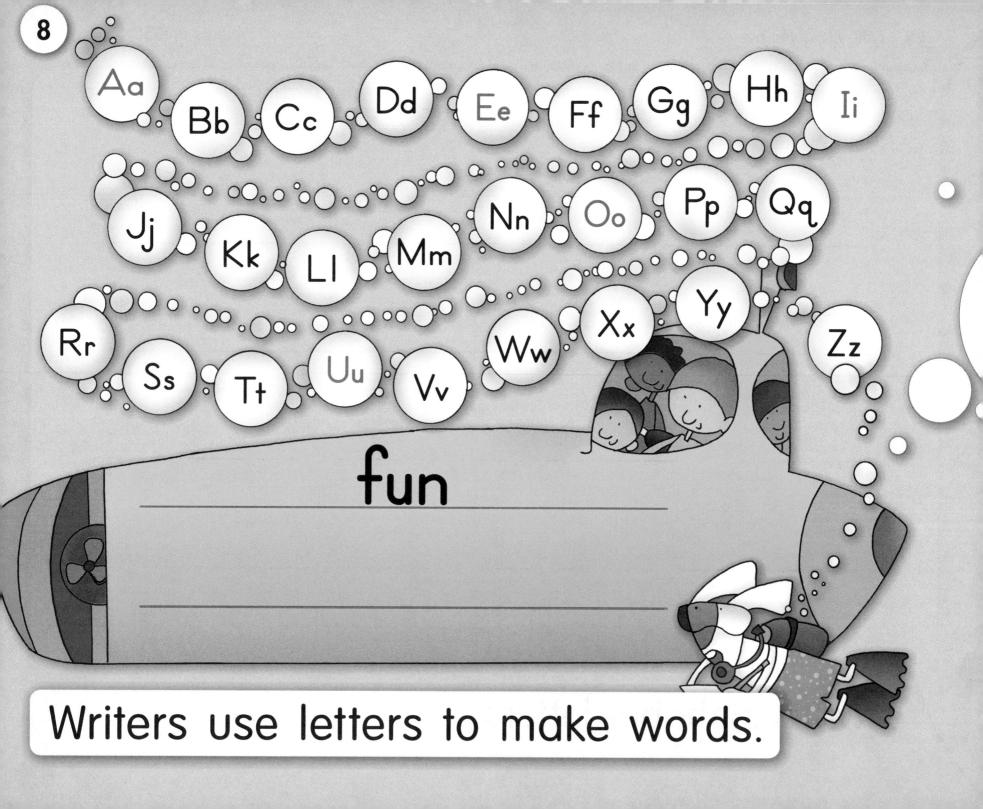

Aa Bb Cc Dd Ee Ff Gg Hh Ii Jj Kk Ll Mm Nn Oo Pp Qq Rr Ss Tt Uu Vv Ww Xx Yy Zz

fun

Writers use letters to make words.

go   like

I use letters to make words.

Spot puts words together.

I can write.

I can _____

I can _____

_____

Writers put words together in sentences.

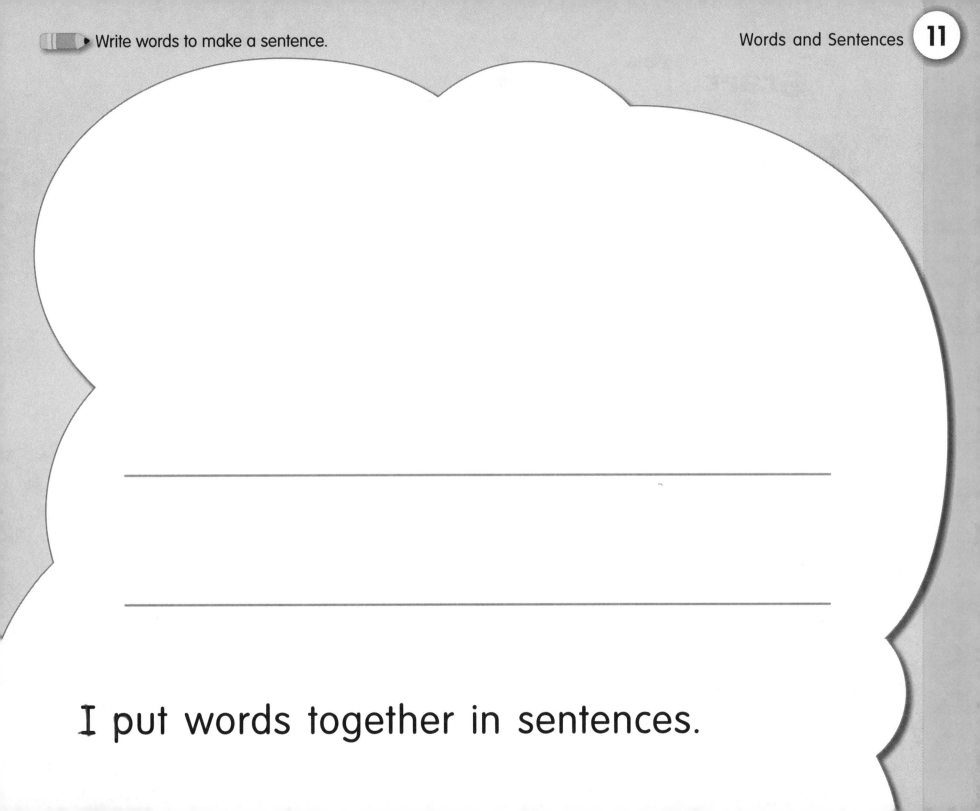

_____

_____

I put words together in sentences.

12

Look at the turtle.

Look at the _____

Writers start sentences with capital letters.

The rabbit runs fast.

He takes a rest.

I start sentences with capital letters.

The turtle walks**.**

Does he stop**?**

No, he never rests**!**

Writers finish sentences with end marks.

The turtle is happy

Where is the rabbit

Here he comes

I finish sentences with end marks.

See **L**ee jump.

Sometimes **I** jump, too.

See _____ jump.

Sometimes____ jump, too.

_____

Writers use capital letters for special words.

_____

_____

_____

I use capital letters for special words.

Alligator sits,
Butterfly flits.

Igloo white,
Jacket bright.

Cup of tea,
Duck at sea.

Kite in the sky,
Ladybug shy.

Eggs to cook,
Fish in a brook.

Mouse near a hole,
Nest like a bowl.

Girl named Mary,
Hat for Harry.

Writers have fun with words.

Octopus below,
Penguin in the snow.

Quilt for a bed,
Rocket that's red.

Socks for running,
Turtle goes sunning.

Umbrella for showers,
Vase full of flowers.

Wagon to pull,
Box full of wool.

Yarn soft and blue,
Zipper-dee-do!

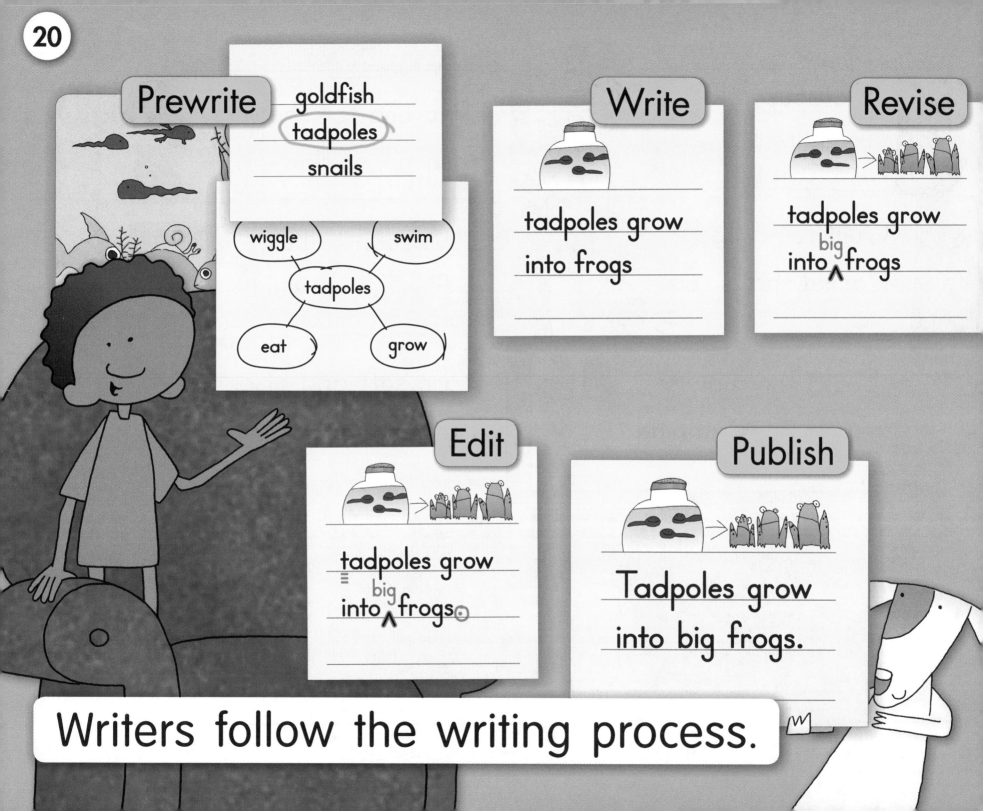

Writers follow the writing process.

Writers look and think to find ideas.

Topic List

goldfish

tadpoles

snails

Writers list words to find a topic.

Writers read to learn.

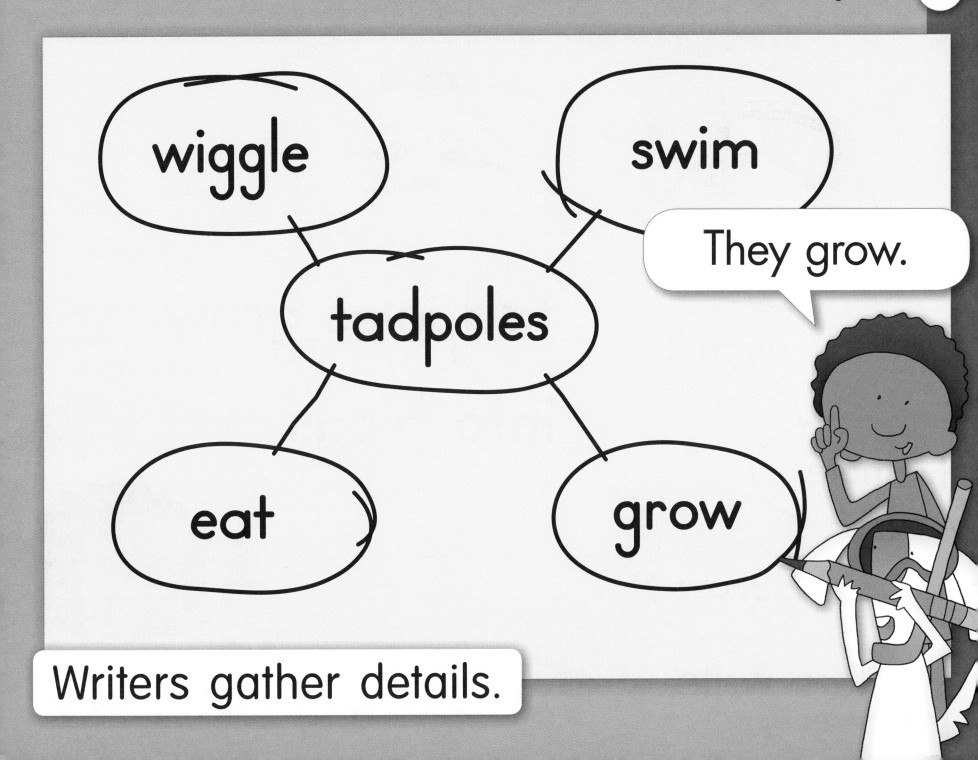

Writers gather details.

26

swim

tadpoles

grow

Writers write.

tadpoles grow
into frogs

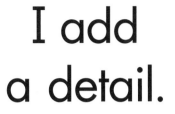

I add a detail.

tadpoles grow

into ∧ frogs
big

Writers add details.

tadpoles grow big into frogs.

Capital letters
Spaces
End marks

Writers check their writing.

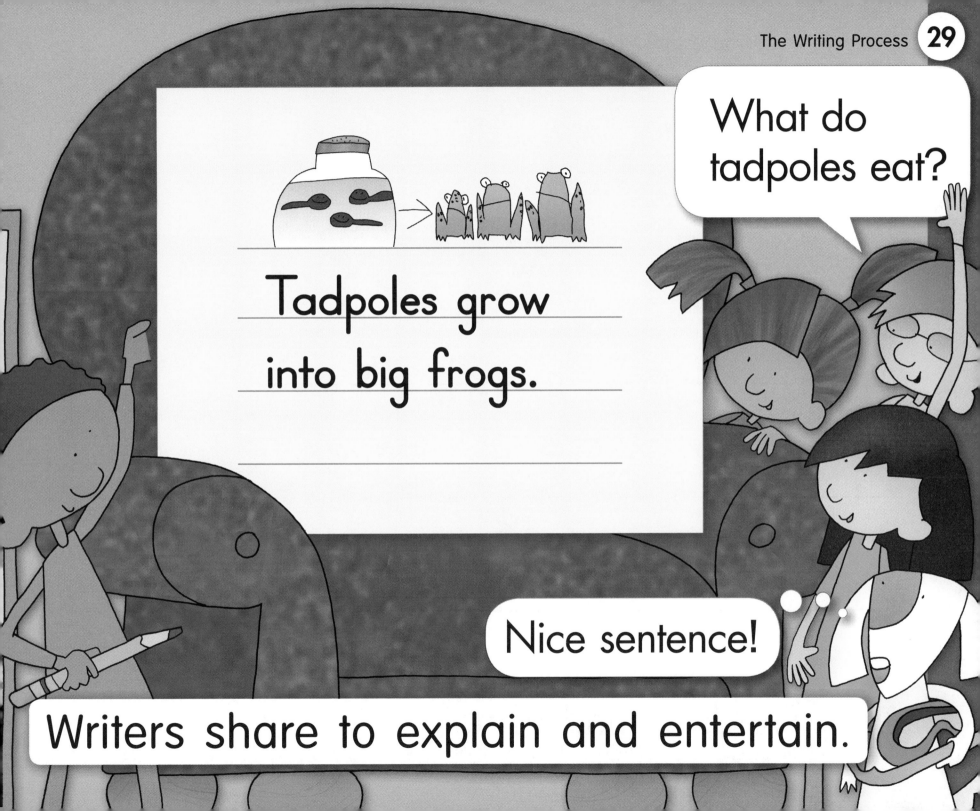

List the names of different animals.

Topic List

_____

_____

_____

I list words to find a topic.

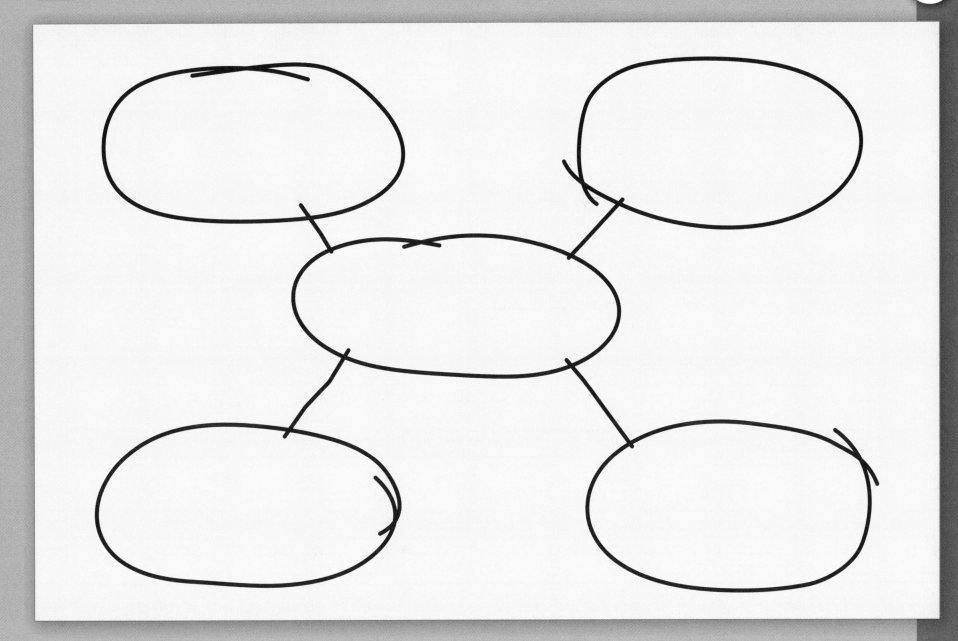

I gather details.

32

Write a sentence using the ideas in your cluster. Then revise and edit your sentence.

_____

_____

_____

I write.

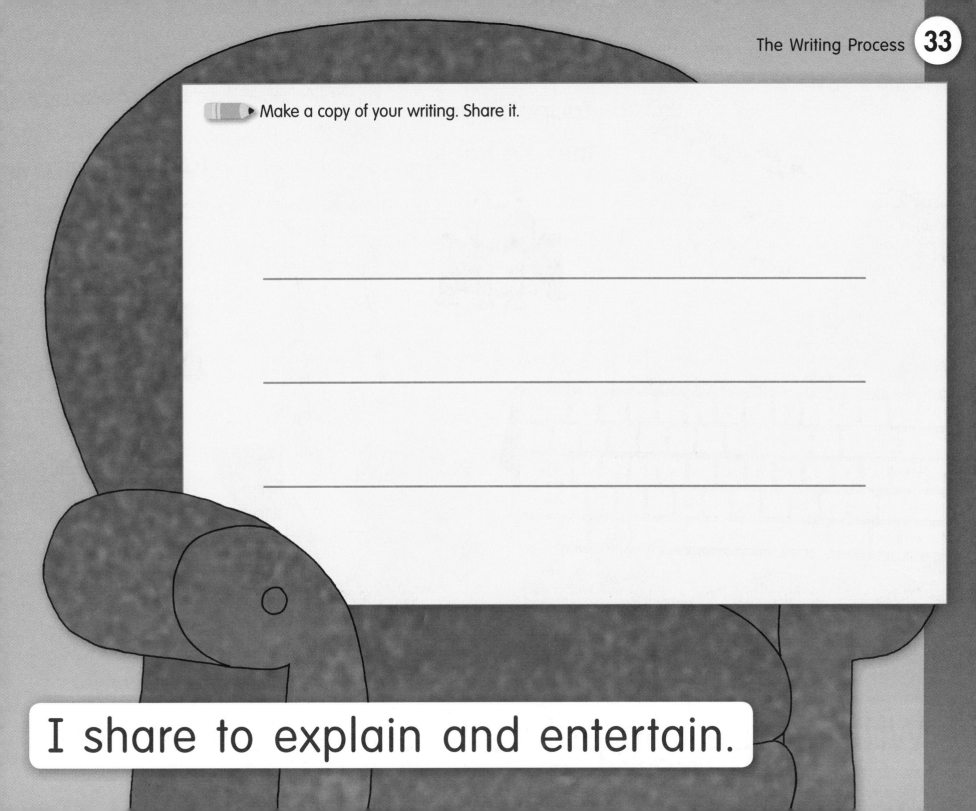

Make a copy of your writing. Share it.

_____

_____

_____

I share to explain and entertain.

Writers use computers to share their writing.

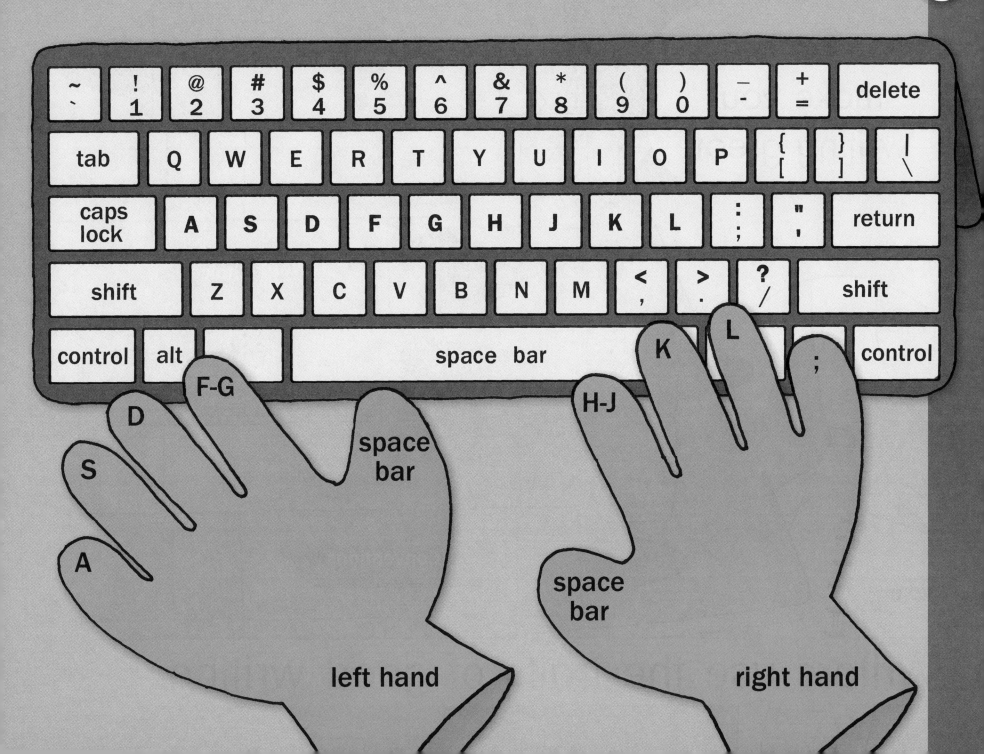

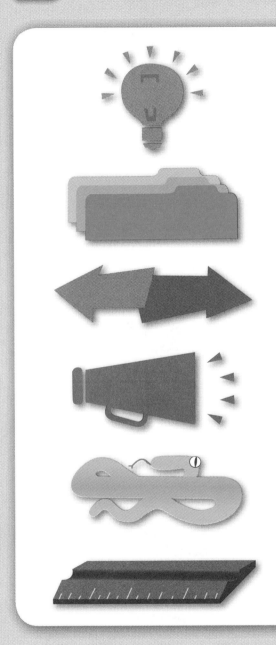

Word Choice

Ideas

Organization

Voice

Conventions

Sentence Fluency

I learn about the traits of good writing.

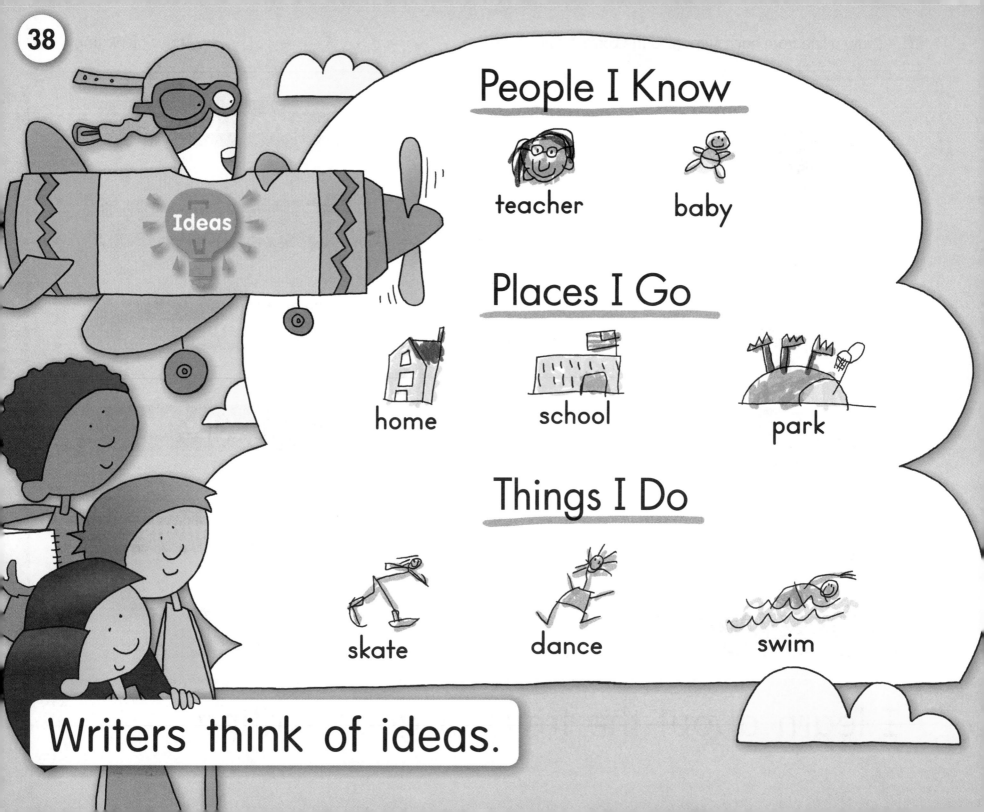

People I Know

teacher   baby

Places I Go

home   school   park

Things I Do

skate   dance   swim

Writers think of ideas.

Ideas

People I Know

Places I Go

Things I Do

I think of ideas.

First

Next

Last

Organization

Writers plan their writing.

Put this story in the correct order. Write the number 1, 2, or 3 above each picture.

I plan my writing.

Organization

42

tweet
boom
crunch

spicy
sour
salty

pink
tiny
pretty

bumpy
wet
hard

smokey
sweet
flowery

Word Choice

hear   taste   see   touch   smell

Writers use their senses.

hear	
taste	
see	
touch	
smell	

Word Choice

I use my senses.

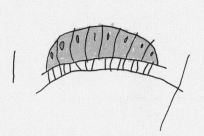 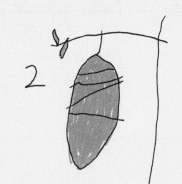 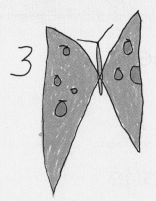

look at the butterfly.

Conventions

Writers follow writing rules.

- ☑ Capital letters
- ☑ Spaces
- ☑ End marks

Conventions

the butterfly is pretty

I follow writing rules.

☐ Capital letters

☐ Spaces

☐ End marks

Writers write in journals.

I write in journals.

Writers make lists.

I make lists.

Writers make signs and labels.

Make a sign in the big space.
Write a label in the small space.

I make signs and labels.

Writers write notes and cards.

Write a note and write on the front of the card. Draw pictures, too.

I write notes and cards.

I play with Kara.

Writers write captions.

I write a caption.

Today's News

Date: _April 6_

News: _Mr. Moss came_

to school today. He is a

TV weather reporter.

Writers write the news.

Today's News

Date: _____

News: _____

_____

_____

_____

I write the news.

Month:

Date:

Fox was singing. Then Bear started dancing. They had fun.

Writers write stories.

I write stories.

Draw some pictures of workers in your community. Write a label.

Themes **61**

Community

day

night

afternoon

morning

evening

sunrise

sunset

Time

▸ Write a time word and draw a picture to go with it.

Time

Colors

Draw a picture using your favorite color. Write its name.

Colors

triangle

circle

rectangle

square

Shapes

Draw a picture using shapes. Label the shapes you use.

Shapes

68

cloud

ice

ocean

lake

pond

stream

river

Water

Draw something you do or see in the water. Write a caption.

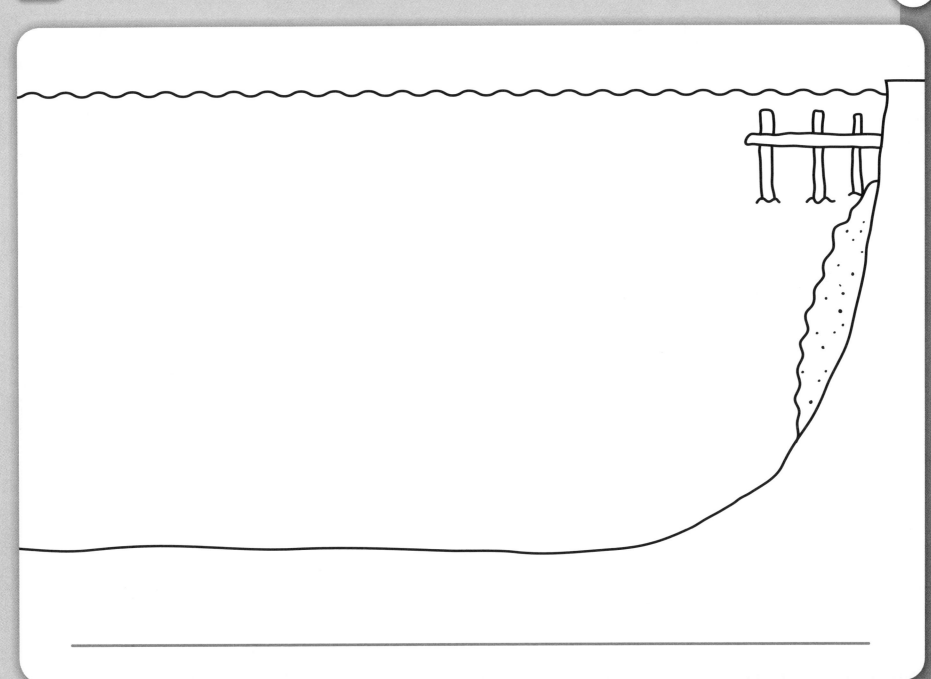

Water

Weather

Draw and label the kind of weather you like.

Weather

TEMPERATURE

°F

Feelings

Make a picture that shows how you feel. Write the feeling word.

Feelings

Make a list of foods you like. Draw some of them.

Food

Write about how you exercise. Draw a picture, too.

Exercise

Location Words

Draw an animal in a place. Use a location word in a sentence about your picture.

Location Words

80

I **hear** with my ears,

I **taste** with my tongue,

I **see** with my eyes
by the light of the sun.

I **touch** with my hands,
along with my toes,

And whatever I **smell**
tickles my nose.

touch

see

taste

hear

smell

The Five Senses

Draw a picture of you using one of your senses. Label it.

The Five Senses

My Word Dictionary

Aa

all

am

and

alligator

Bb

be

but

by

butterfly

Cc

can

cat

come

cup

Dd

dad

did

do

duck

Ee

ear

eat

eye

eggs

Ff

for

friend

from

fish

Gg

get

go

good

girl

Hh

had

have

he

hat

I i

in

is

it

igloo

J j

jar

jump

just

jacket

Kk

keep
kind
know

kite

Ll

let
like
little

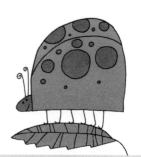

ladybug

Mm

mouse

me

mom

my

Nn

nest

no

not

now

Oo

of

on

or

octopus

Pp

play

please

put

penguin

Qq

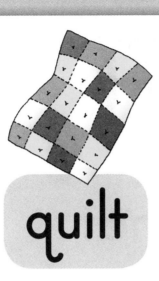

quick

quiet

quit

quilt

Rr

ran

read

run

rocket

Ss

see

she

so

socks

Tt

that

the

they

turtle

Uu

up

us

use

umbrella

Vv

van

very

vet

vase

Ww

was

we

with

wagon

Xx

x-ray

fox

wax

box

Yy

yes

you

your

yarn

Zz

zero

zip

zoo

zipper

My name is

Spot

I can write these names.